One Million and One
The OUR WORLD Series

1,000,001
Ways To Go To School

Connie Goyette Crawley

To Shaun.
Thank you for showing me the world.

**Book 1
of
One Million and One: The OUR WORLD Series**

Published by 3DLight Publications
Fayetteville, GA
Text copyright © 2016
Connie Goyette Crawley

conniecrawley.com

ISBN: 978-0-9986614-1-4
2nd Edition

All rights reserved. This book or parts thereof may not be reproduced in any form, stored in any retrieval system, or transmitted in any form by any means—electronic, mechanical, photocopy, recording, or otherwise—without prior written permission of the publisher, except as provided by United States of America copyright law. For permission requests, contact the publisher via www.conniecrawley.com

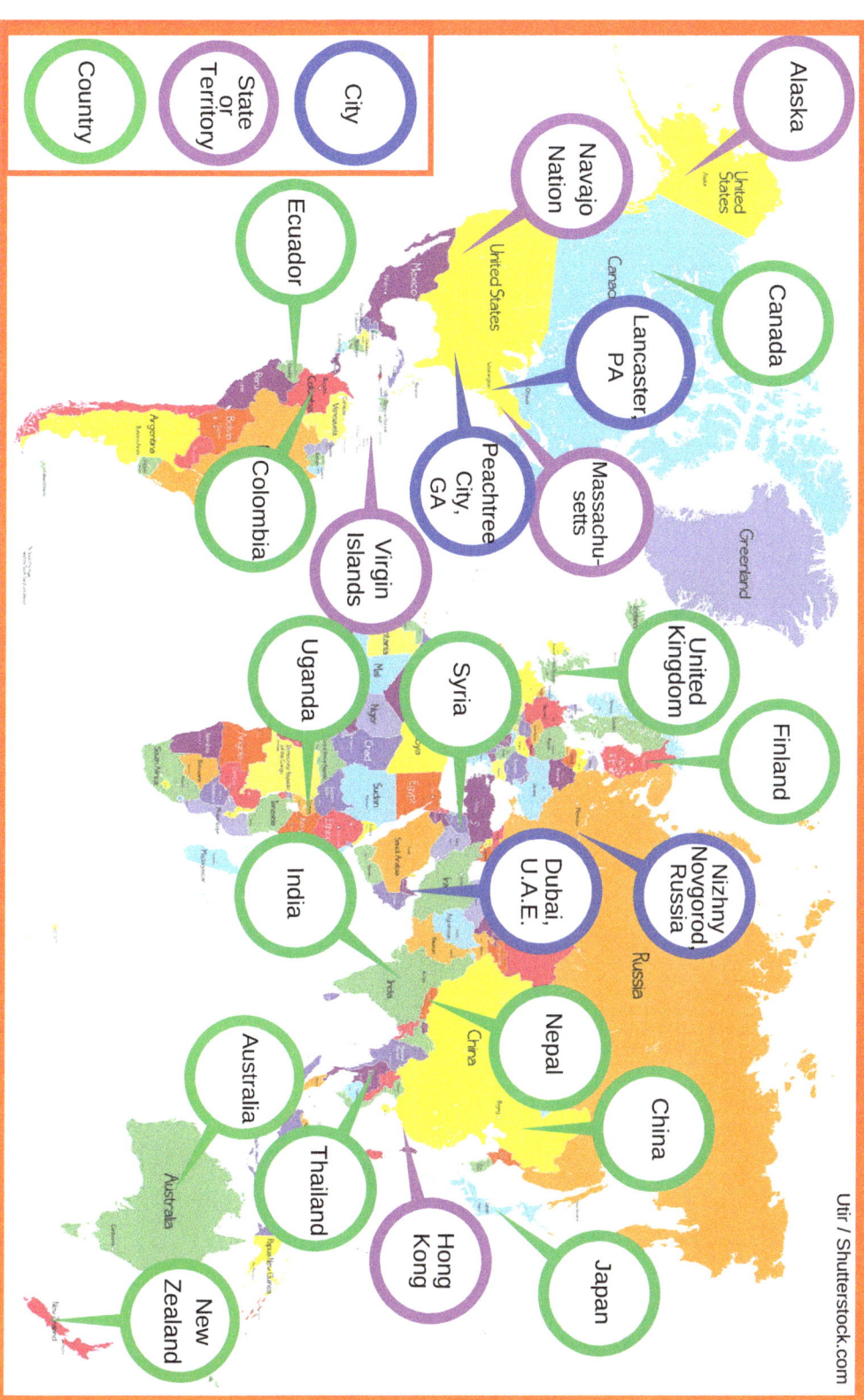

Every minute
of every hour
of almost every day,
somewhere in the world
kids are heading to school.

From cities, and towns, and villages…
From mountains, and deserts and islands…

In all kinds of weather…
Using every imaginable kind of transportation
Over a BILLION kids are heading to school.

Which means...

. . . with all of the students
in all of the places all over the world
who use
every imaginable kind of transportation. . .
There are at least a **million** ways
to go to school.

$$\begin{array}{r} 1{,}000{,}000 \\ +\quad \text{YOU} \\ \hline 1{,}000{,}001 \end{array}$$

Ways To Go To School

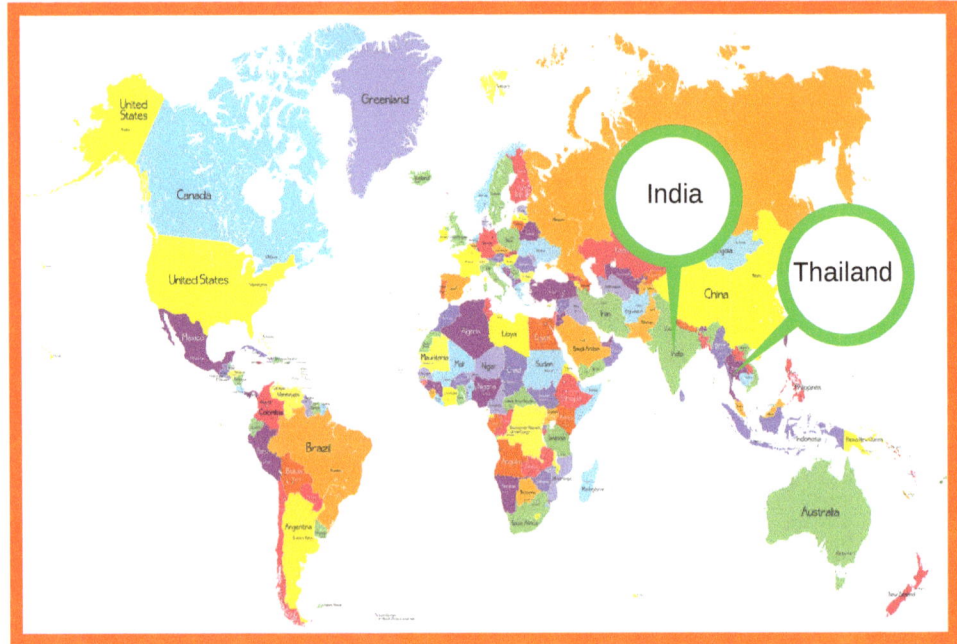

- The Republic of India is one of the world's oldest civilizations and is the world's largest democracy.
- New Delhi is the capital of India.
- The game of chess was invented in India.

- The Kingdom of Thailand is in Southeast Asia.
- The king is the leader of the country and lives in the Grand Palace.
- The capital of Thailand is:

Krungthepmahanakhon Amonrattanakosin Mahintharayutthaya Mahadilokphop Noppharatratchathaniburirom Udomratchaniwetmahasathan Amonphimanawatansathit Sakkathattiyawitsanukamprasit

It is also known as Bangkok.

Rickshaw and Tuk-tuk

A rickshaw is a two or three-wheeled vehicle with a seat for passengers. These children in India ride to school on: **1.** a pulled rickshaw and **2.** a cycle rickshaw. **3.** Tuk-tuks are like rickshaws, but are powered by motors and are named for their puttering sound. These students in Thailand take a tuk-tuk to school.

- The Navajo Nation is a Native American territory in the United States.
- It covers parts of Arizona, New Mexico, and Utah.
- The Navajo Nation has its own government and laws but the Navajo people are also citizens of the United States.

- The Republic of Ecuador is named for the equator, the imaginary line that divides the earth into a northern and southern hemisphere.
- The equator passes through Ecuador.
- Ecuador is the smallest country in South America.
- The capital is of Ecuador is Quito.

Horseback

Students in many different parts of the world ride horses to school. **1.** A horse waits for its rider outside of a school in the Navajo Nation in Arizona. **2.** These sisters in Ecuador ride to school together.

- The Republic of Colombia is the only country in South America that touches both the Pacific Ocean and the Caribbean Sea.
- The capital of Colombia is Bogota.
- Colombia exports more emeralds than any other country.

Zipline

Some children, who live high up in the mountains in Colombia, zip to school! A zipline is a cable and pulley system. Ziplines have been used in the mountains of South America for hundreds of years for transportation and just for fun.

- Nizhny Novgorod is the 5th largest city in Russia.
- The city was built where the Volga and Oka rivers come together.
- Nizhny means "lower".
- Nizhny (lower) Novgorod is usually just called Nizhny, so that it's not confused with "Novgorod the Great", a city in western Russia.

Hovercraft

Some students who live near Nizhny Novgorod in Russia travel by hovercraft across the Volga River to get to school. Hovercrafts float over land, water, mud and ice. Powerful fans blow air to push the hovercraft up so that it floats 6-7 inches above the surface.

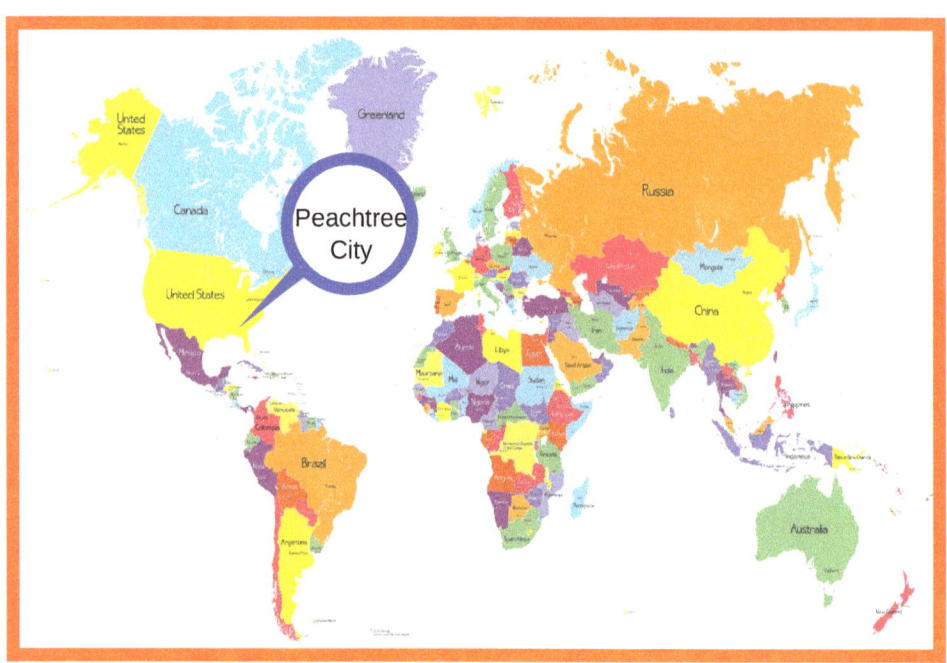

- Peachtree City, Georgia is in the southeastern United States.
- There are more than 90 miles of golf cart paths in Peachtree City, which are used for walking, biking, skating, and jogging.
- Children, who are at least 12 years old, may drive a golf cart with a parent or guardian in the front seat.

Golf Cart

In Peachtree City, Georgia, many students ride to school on golf carts. Here's a crowded golf cart parking lot at a school. Most golf carts are powered by electricity, so they're better for the environment than cars or buses.

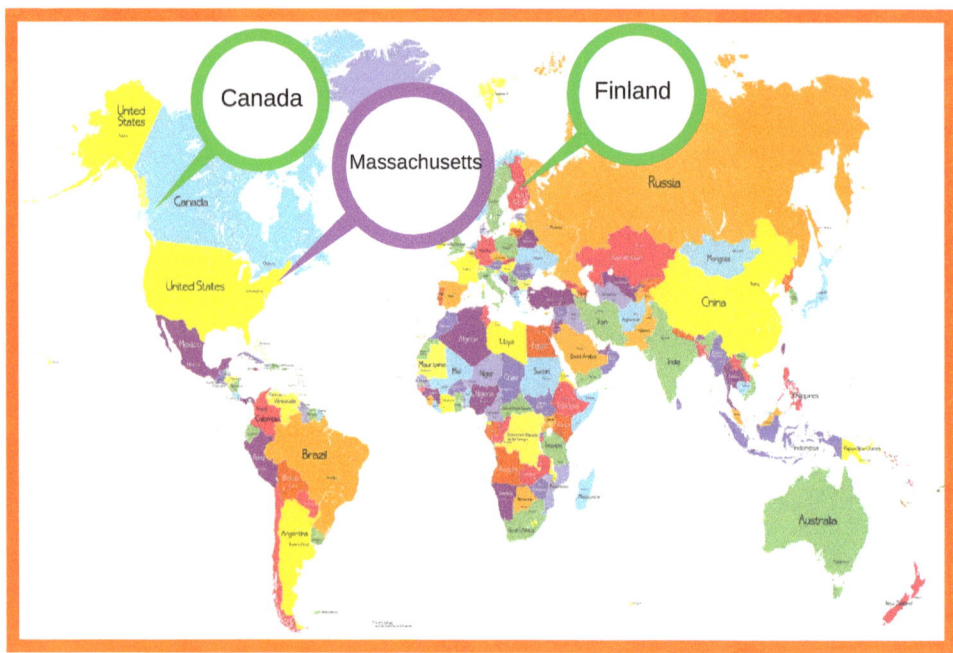

- The Republic of Finland is in northern Europe. It is bordered by Sweden, Russia, and Norway.
- The capital is Helsinki.

- The state of Massachusetts was named after the Massachusetts Native American tribe.
- The game of basketball was invented in Massachusetts.

- Canada is the second largest country in the world.
- Canada has more lakes than all of the rest of the countries in the world combined.
- Both snowmobiles and snow blowers were invented by Canadians.
- The capital of Canada is Ottawa.

Skis, Sleds, and Snowshoes

Students in cold climates go to school in a variety of ways. **1.** Some students in Finland ski to school in the winter. **2.** These kids in Massachusetts can sled down the hill to their school. **3.** In some places in Canada, students snowshoe to school.

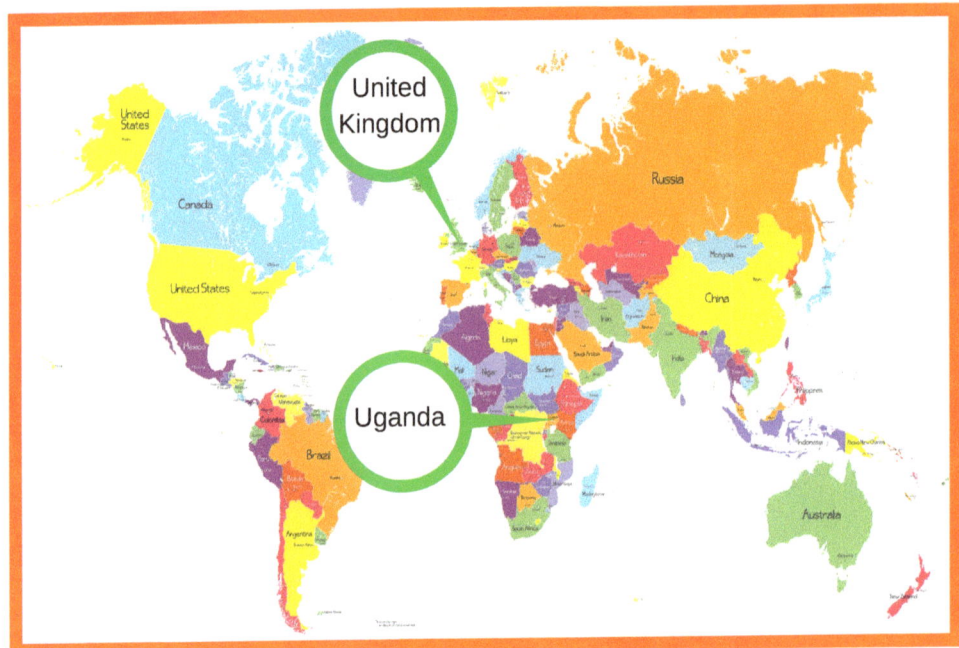

- The United Kingdom of Great Britain and Northern Ireland (UK) is made up of the countries of England, Scotland, Wales, and Northern Ireland.
- The Channel Tunnel connects the UK to France. It is 23.5 miles long and is the world's longest underground tunnel. It is often called the "Chunnel".

- Uganda is a country in eastern Africa and is sometimes called the "Pearl of Africa".
- Uganda is on the equator.
- The capital of Uganda is Kampala.
- More than half of the world's endangered mountain gorillas are in Uganda.

Scooter and Bike

1. These scooters are parked at a school in Great Britain. Scooters are used by both children and adults for fast, easy transportation. **2.** There are over one billion bicycles in the world about twice as many bikes as motor vehicles. These students bike to school in the East African country of Uganda.

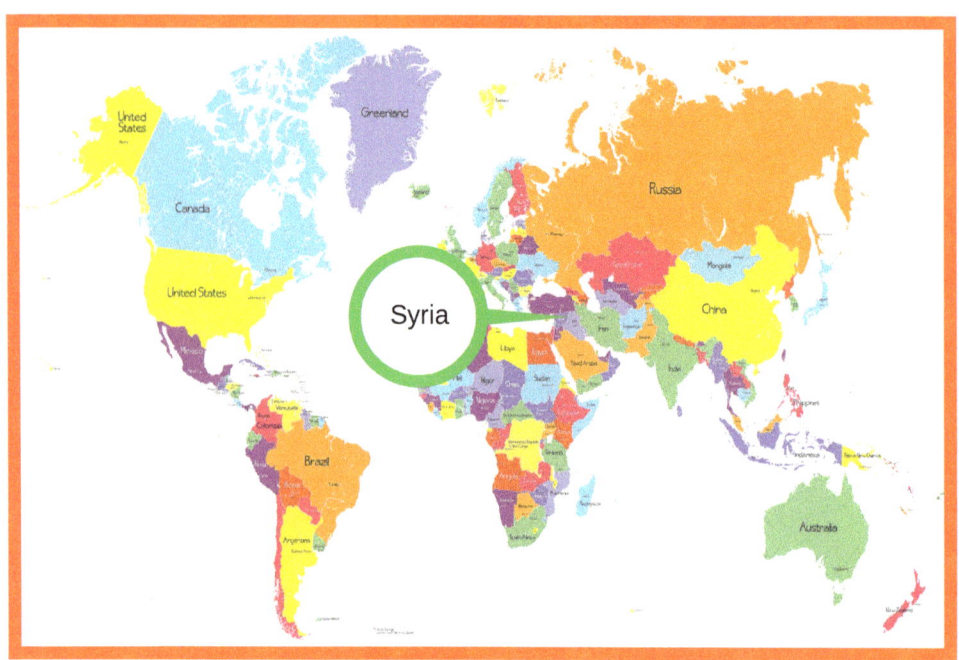

- The Syrian Arab Republic is home to one of the world's oldest civilizations.
- Damascus, the capital of Syria, is believed to be the oldest continually inhabited city in the world.
- The ruins of the ancient city of Palmyra are about 150 miles from Damascus.
- Palmyra was on an important trade route linking Persia (now called Iran), India, and China with the Roman Empire.

Camel

Camels have been used for transportation in the desert for thousands of years. These boys in Syria ride past the ruins of the ancient city of Palmyra on their way to school.

- Alaska was purchased from Russia in 1867 for 2 cents per acre – a total of about 7 million dollars.
- Alaska became a state in 1959 and is the largest state in the United States.
- Alaska's state sport is dog mushing, which involves a team of dogs pulling a sled.

ATVs

These Alaskan children get a fast ride to school on an all-terrain vehicle, also known as an "ATV". ATVs are off-road vehicles and are used for driving through snow and mud. In Alaska, some older students drive their own ATVs to school.

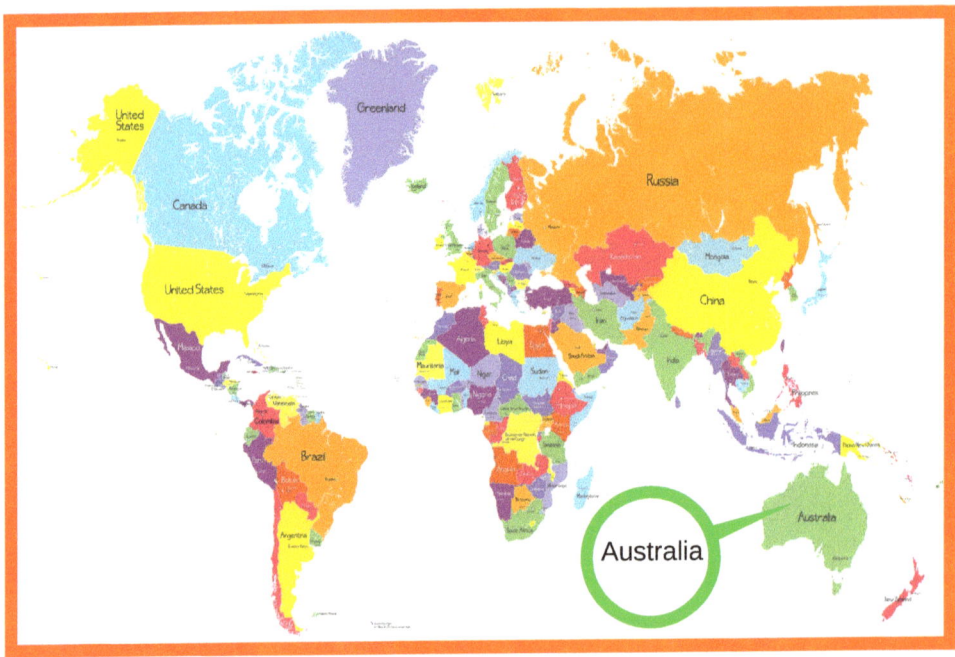

- Australia is both a country and a continent.
- The official name of the country is the Commonwealth of Australia, which also includes the island of Tasmania and other smaller islands.
- Australia is the 6th largest country in the world.
- The capital of Australia is Canberra.
- The Australian outback is the large, semi-desert part of Australia - far from most cities and towns.

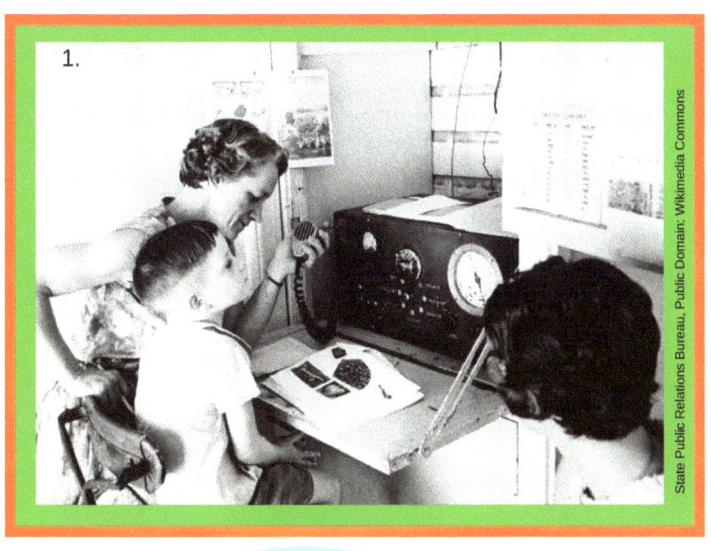

Online School
Some students in Australia live over 500 miles from the closest school so they attend Australia's School of the Air. **1.** Years ago, classes were held over the radio. **2.** Today, students attend classes online using a web cam. Teachers also visit students at home.

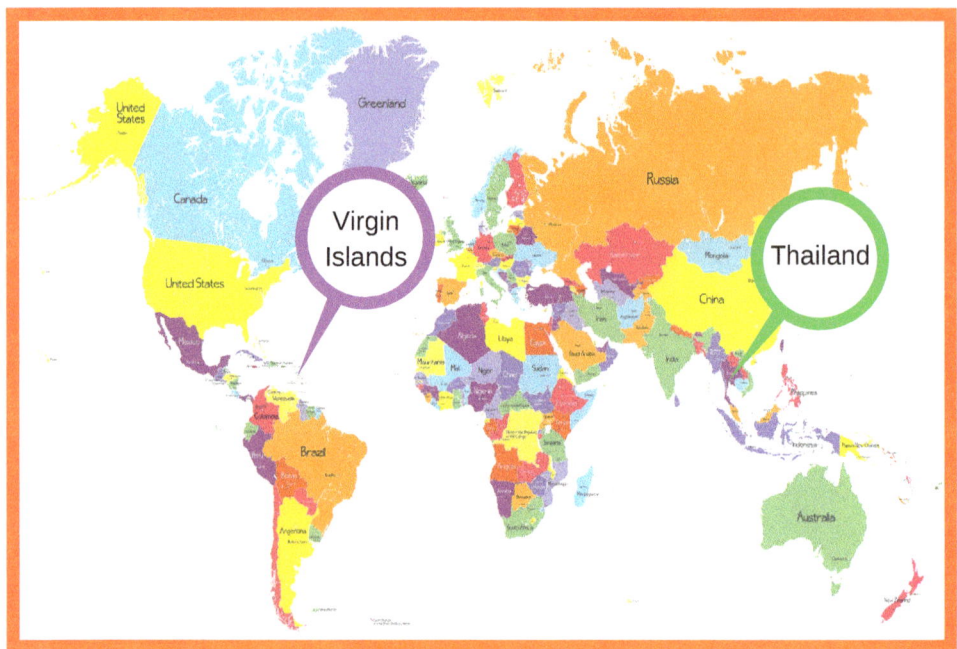

- Thailand, which means "land of the free", was known as Siam until 1939.
  (See page 4 for more information about Thailand.)

- The Virgin Islands are a group of islands in the Caribbean – divided into the United States Virgin Islands and the British Virgin Islands.
- The U.S. Virgin Islands of St. Thomas, St. John, St. Croix, and 50 minor islands are a U.S. territory.
- U.S. Virgin Islands residents are U.S. citizens, but do not vote in presidential elections.
- The main British Virgin Islands are Tortola, Virgin Gorda, Anegada, and Jost Van Dyke.

Ferry

Students in many parts of the world, including both
1. Thailand and
2. the Virgin Islands, live on one island and attend school on another. Ferries like these take students back and forth from one island to the other.

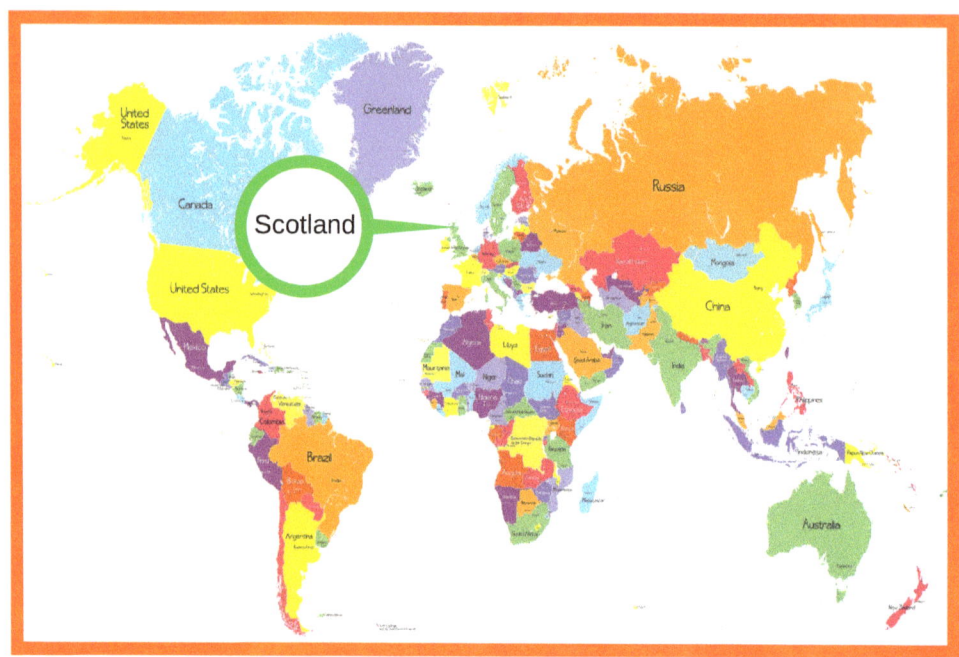

- Scotland is a part of the United Kingdom (UK) which also includes England, Wales, and Northern Ireland.
- The capital of Scotland is Edinburgh.
- There are 790 islands off the coast of Scotland.
- The Shetland Islands and Orkney Islands were once part of Norway.

Airplane

When ferries aren't available, children who live on the island of Papa Westray, in the Orkney Islands off the coast of Scotland, take one of the shortest flights in the world to go to school.

The flight is just one mile and takes 96 seconds.

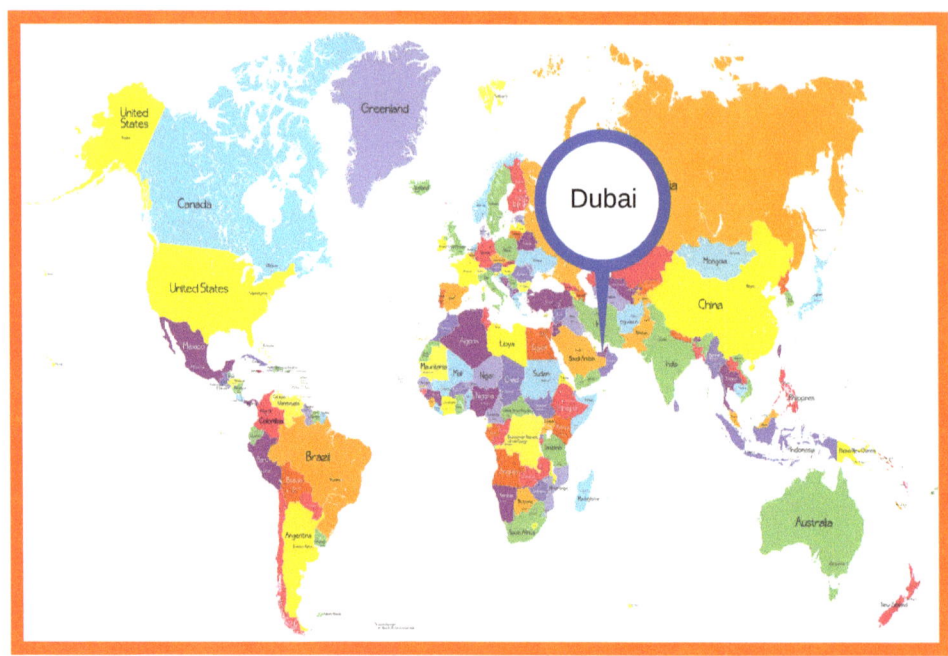

- Dubai is the largest city in the United Arab Emirates (U.A.E.).
- The U.A.E. is a group of seven emirates, which are like states or provinces.
- Each emirate is ruled by an Emir.
- The tallest building in the world, the Burj Khalifa, which has 164 floors, is in Dubai.

Abra

An abra is a wooden boat. The driver sits in the center of the abra with the passengers sitting around him, facing the water. In Dubai, a city in the United Arab Emirates, some students use abras to cross Dubai Creek on their way to school. The trip takes just a few minutes.

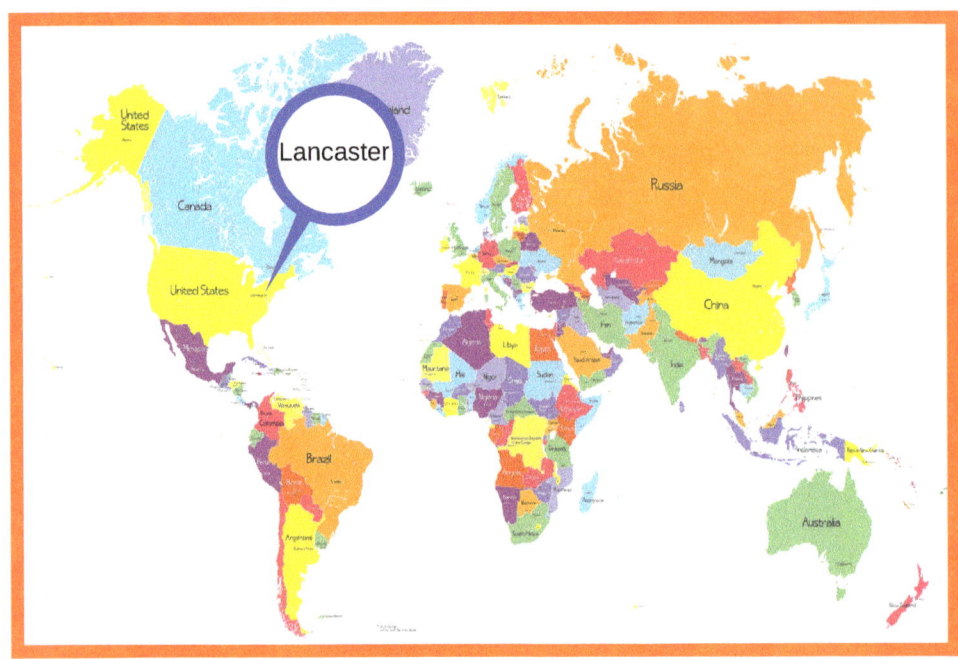

- Lancaster, Pennsylvania is one of the oldest inland towns in the United States.
- Lancaster was originally called Hickory Town.
- During the American Revolutionary War, Lancaster was the capital of the United States for one day, September 27, 1777, after Philadelphia was captured by the British.

Horse and Buggy
Many people of the Amish faith live near Lancaster, Pennsylvania. Since most Amish people don't drive cars or use other modern technology, Amish children ride to school in a horse and buggy. Many Amish children only attend school through the 8th grade.

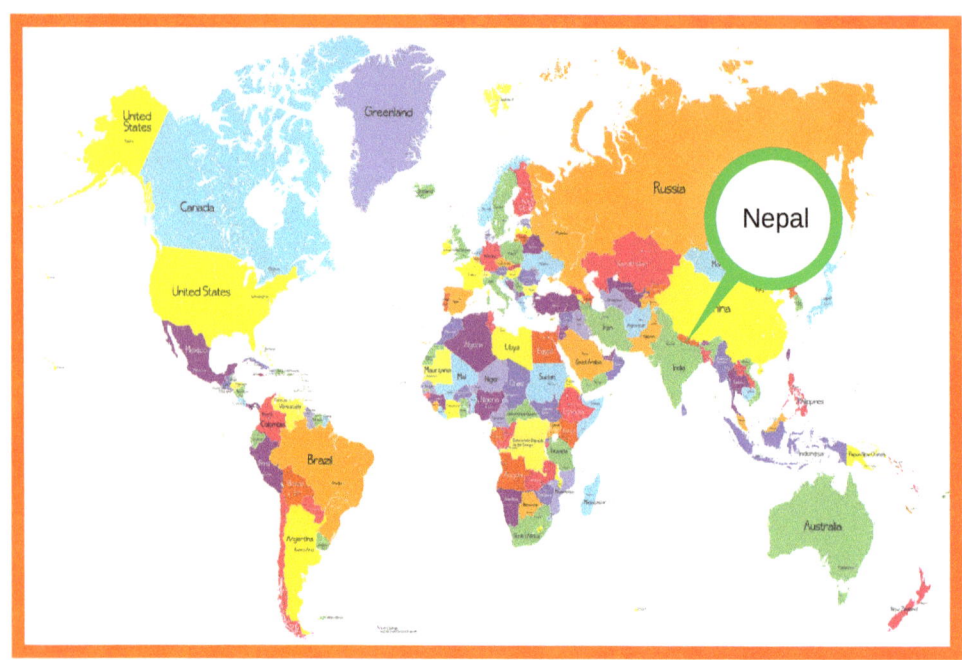

- The Federal Democratic Republic of Nepal is bordered by China and India.
- The capital of Nepal is Kathmandu.
- The Himalayan Mountain chain runs through Nepal.
- Eight out of the ten highest mountains in the world are in Nepal, including Mount Everest, the world's highest mountain.

Cable Car

These students in Nepal use a tuin to cross a river on their way to school. A tuin is a hand-powered cable car used to cross a river when there is not a bridge nearby. People sit or stand in the basket and pull themselves along or are pulled by ropes from the other side.

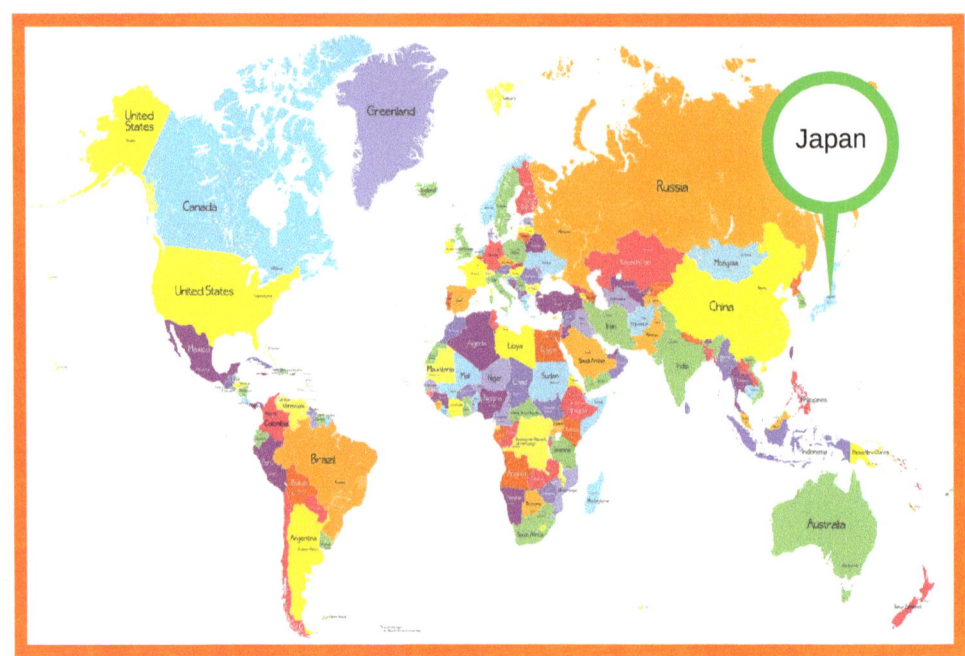

- Japan is an island nation in East Asia.
- It is made up of 6,852 islands.
- The capital of Japan is Tokyo, which is on Honshu, the largest island.
- The highest point in Japan is Mount Fuji, which is over 12,000 feet tall.
- Japan is the only country in the world with a reigning emperor. The emperor has no real power, but is an important symbol of the country.

Bullet Train

Some students in Japan, who travel long distances to go to school, ride a bullet train. Bullet trains are called shinkansen, which means "New Trunk Line". Bullet trains travel at over 200 miles per hour!

Walking and riding a bus are the two most common ways for students to go to school.

See if you can guess where each of these school bus pictures was taken.

Turn the page to see the answers!

1. U.S.A.
United States of America
Capital: Washington D.C.

About 26 million U.S. students ride a school bus to school.

2. New Zealand
Capital: Wellington

New Zealanders often refer to themselves as "kiwis". A kiwi is a flightless bird, and is a symbol of New Zealand.

Many school buses in New Zealand are red.

3. China
People's Republic of China
Capital: Beijing

China has the largest population of any country in the world.

4. Hong Kong
Hong Kong is an island in China's Special Administrative Region, a territory between mainland China and the South China Sea. It is part of China, but has its own legal system, government, and money.

See our award-winning books and get free printables
at
conniecrawley.com!

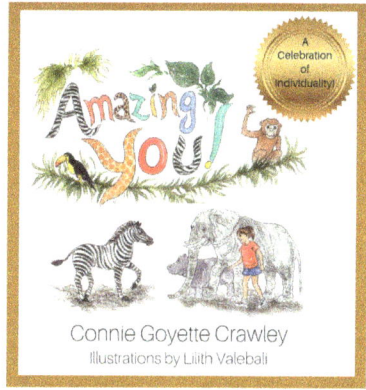

Easy-As-Pie Chapter Books starring Tilly and Torg!

Book Readers Appreciation Group Medallion Winner!

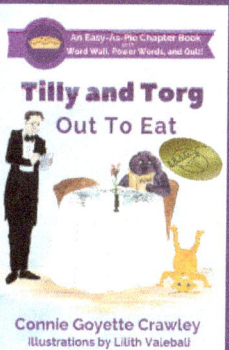  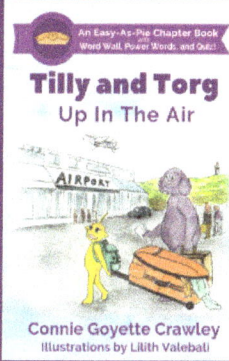 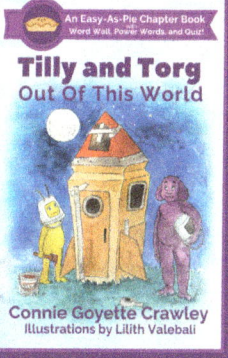

One Million and One: The OUR WORLD Series
A non-fiction series featuring amazing photographs, colorful maps, fun facts, and research & quiz questions!

eLit Award and National Indie Excellence Award Winners

Connie Crawley is a former elementary school teacher,
a consultant for an educational software company,
and an award-winning author.

She's grateful for all the people in her life,
and to have had the chance to
explore the world with her husband, Shaun.

**Find out more and get free printable resources
at conniecrawley.com**

Research Questions

Look back through the book to find the answers to these questions:

1. What city is believed to be the oldest continually inhabited city in the world? What country is it in?

2. Which country has more lakes than all of the rest of the countries in the world combined?

3. What is the highest mountain in the world? What country is it in?

4. Thailand was known as _____ until 1939.

5. What is the smallest country in South America?

6. What is an emirate?

7. Where was chess invented?

8. More than half of the world's mountain gorillas live in _____.

9. Alaska was purchased from Russia in _____. It became a state in _____.

10. _____ is both a country and a continent.

More research questions and a printable map available to download FREE at conniecrawley.com.

Copyright

Cover bus: Carlos E. Santa Maria / Shutterstock.com

1. Utir / Shutterstock.com

5. a. By Arne Hückelheim - Own work, CC BY-SA 3.0, https://commons.wikimedia.org/w/index.php?curid=15474889 Ae Hückelheim - CC BY-SA 3.0, Wikicommons
   b. Mikhail Hoboton Popov / Shutterstock.com
   c. By http://www.flickr.com/ photos/txd/ (http://www.flickr.com/photos/txd/2681200611/) [CC BY 2.0 (http://creativecommons.org/licenses/by/2.0)], via Wikimedia Commons

7. a. Joseph Sohm/Shutterstock.com
   b. DFLC Prints / Shutterstock.com

9. a. education-for-solidarity.blogspot.com/2013
   b. Pixabay: CC0 1.0 Universal (CC0 1.0)
   c. Khaufle http://www.gnu.org/copyleft/fdl.html CC-BY-SA-3.0 (http://creativecommons.org/licenses/by-sa/3.0/)], via Wikimedia

11. Pictures by Shirokov Oleg / Logoprom.ru (Own work) [CC BY CA 3.0 http://creativecommons.org /licenses/by-sa/3.0)], via Wikimedia Commons

13. a. sonya etchison / Shutterstock.com
    b. Golf cart parking by Tony Bernard / Flickr / (CC-BY-SA 2.0)

15. a. By Anneli Salo (Own work) [CC BY-SA 3.0 (http://creativecommons.org/licenses/by-sa/3.0)], via Wikimedia Commons https://commons.wikimedia.org/wiki/File%3AChildren_skiing_IMG_3920.JPG
    b. Photo courtesy of Molly Maginnis Butler.
    c. Snowshoes two styles by Burtonpe / Wikicommons / CC-BY-SA-3.0

17. a. Turibamwe / pixabay.com CC0 – public domain
    b. Ed Yourdon CC BY-SA 2.0 Wikimedia Commons Image Copyright Chris Reynolds. This work is licensed under the Creative Commons Attribution-Share Alike 2.0 Generic Licence. To view a copy of this licence, visit http://creativecommons.org/licenses/by-sa/2.0/ or send a letter to Creative Commons, 171 Second Street, Suite 300, San Francisco, California, 94105, USA.

19. a. seb001 / Shutterstock.com
    b. Pixabay / Marie France CC0 Public Domain

21. Kent Harville / Eskimo Children Enjoy 'Arctic Edge' Adventure Baptist Press July, 2006 Used by permission: Lifeway Christian Resources

23. a. Photo by Premier's Department, State Public Relations Bureau, Photographic Unit [Public domain], via Wikimedia Commons
    b. Jacek Chabraszewski / Shutterstock.com

25. a. 1000 Words / Shutterstock.com
    b. Cruz Bay: By FloNight (Sydney Poore) and Russell Poore (Own work by Russell and Sydney Poore) [CC BY-SA 3.0 (http://creativecommons.org/licenses/by-sa/3.0) or GFDL (http://www.gnu.org/copyleft/fdl.html)], via Wikimedia Commons

27. Image by Orkney Photographic. Used by permission.

29. a. dvoevnore / Shutterstock.com
    b. https://en.wikipedia.org/wiki/File:Dubai-abra1.JPG CC BY 2.5, https://en.wikipedia.org/w/index.php?curid=10793032

31. a. hutch photography / Shutterstock.com
    b. By it:Utente:TheCadExpert (it:Immagine:Lancaster_County_Amish_03.jpg) [GFDL (http://www.gnu.org/copyleft/fdl.html) or CC-BY-SA-3.0 (http://creativecommons.org/licenses/by-sa/3.0/)], via Wikimedia Commons

33. Pictures by Appropedia user "Steven M." [CC BY-SA 3.0 (http://creativecommons.org/licenses/by-sa/3.0/)], via Wikimedia Commons

35. a. Sakarin Sawasdinaka / Shutterstock.com
    b. cowardlion / Shutterstock.com

37. a. ebpilgrim / pixabay.com CC0 – public domain
    b. Matthew25187   / Wikicommons / CC-BY-SA-3.0
    c. By Ed Webster (original), cropped by User:Ultra7 [CC BY 2.0 (http://creativecommons.org/licenses/by/2.0)], via Wikimedia Commons
    d. By Michael Tyler (Flickr: Big Yellow Bus) [CC BY-SA 2.0 (http://creativecommons.org/licenses/by-sa/2.0)], via Wikimedia Commons

www.ingramcontent.com/pod-product-compliance
Lightning Source LLC
Chambersburg PA
CBHW040331300426
44113CB00020B/2723